COOKERY AMERICANA

H. M. KINSLEY

ONE HUNDRED RECIPES FOR THE CHAFING DISH

Introduction and Suggested Recipes

by

LOUIS SZATHMÁRY

Creative Cookbooks
An imprint of Fredonia Books
Amsterdam, The Netherlands

One Hundred Recipes
for the Chafing Dish

by
H. M. Kinsley

Introduction and suggested recipes by
Louis Szathmáry

ISBN 1-58963-034-3

Copyright © 2001 by Fredonia Books

Reprinted from the 1973 edition

Creative Cookbooks
An imprint of
Fredonia Books
Amsterdam, The Netherlands
http://www.FredoniaBooks.com

COOKERY AMERICANA is a series of 27 cookbooks in 15 volumes that chronicles a fascinating aspect of American social life over the past 150 years. These volumes provide unique insight into the American experience and follow the movement of pioneer America from the original colonies to the Great Plains and westward to the Pacific. More than cookbooks, these works were manuals for daily living: household management, etiquette, home medicinal remedies, and much more. See the last pages of this volume for a complete listing of the series.

LOUIS I. SZATHMARY, Advisory Editor for this series, is an internationally known chef, food management consultant, owner of the renowned Chicago restaurant, The Bakery, and author of the best selling *The Chef's Secret Cookbook* (Quadrangle Books, 1971). As a serious student of the history of cookery, he has collected a library of several thousand cookbooks dating back to the 15th century. All of the works in *Cookery Americana* are from his private collection.

Introduction

If one glances or thumbs through another volume in this series, *The Kansas Home Cook-Book* (Arno Press, 1973), and then spends time with this delightful, little book, he will soon notice that with this book a natural shift in emphasis had occurred, as interest moved from the kitchen into the dining room, from preparing food for the family to serving and entertaining guests, and from seeking the bare necessities to desiring the finer things in life.

The Civil War had ended only a generation before, and in only a few more years the twentieth century and a definite "new age" would arrive. It had been only a few years since the first telephone call, and also a few years since the first automobile was offered for sale to the public. The whole American continent was on the move. Americans were looking for the better things in life, so a large silver manufacturing company found it worthwhile to publish a lovely cookbook with some 100 recipes based only on chafing dish cookery.

An attempt was made to put the chafing dish into a historical and cultural context by tracing its history from the ancient Greeks and Romans, to the Middle Ages, into the Age of Discovery, and finally bringing it to the New World in 1720. According to the

1

Introduction, "The colonists having overcome the difficulties incidental upon the making of a new country, began to appreciate and to desire the luxuries and adornments of refined living."

For lack of the chafing dish, a certain French minister suffered mortification by the caustic wit of Talleyrand. The fish, when served to Talleyrand, was cold. " 'That is a magnificent carp,' said the financier, 'how do you like it? It came from my estate in Virsur Ainse.' 'Did it?' said Talleyrand. 'But why did you not have it cooked here?' "

After reassuring the reader that the sincerest expression of hospitality is to serve with chafing dishes, a long list of useful and not-so-useful recipes is given. Some of them are still as excellent today as they were when the book was written. Among those worth trying are the ones we have translated for the modern cook— Crab Meat à la Newburgh (p. 52), Liver à la Suisse (p. 108), and Rum Omelette (p. 129).

It is interesting to note that the book attempts to give accurate measurements and accurate timings, explaining the conditions under which the dishes were prepared in the company's testing facilities. Although many of the entries are very elegant party dishes or restaurant-type dishes, such as those recipes which use lobster, crab, oysters and steak, the author also includes wholesome, but very simple dishes such as Frankfurter and Cabbage (p. 158), Welsh Rarebit (p. 178) and Smoked Pigs Jowl (p. 97).

The pictures in the book show nothing of the food, but the chafing dishes themselves are beautifully displayed.

The author, H. M. Kinsley, was not a static person. He worked at such restaurants as the *Holland House* in New York and *Kins-*

ley's in Chicago. Thus, he moved from working for someone else to owning a business of his own, moving from the East to the center of the country with a definite eye on eventually conquering the rest of the country.

Louis Szathmáry
CHICAGO, ILLINOIS

SUGGESTED RECIPES

The following recipes have been tested and adjusted to today's ingredients, measurements, and style of cooking by Chef Louis Szathmáry.

CRAB MEAT A LA NEWBURGH (p. 52)

INGREDIENTS FOR 8:
1 portion White Sauce*
2 7½-ounce cans crab meat
White pepper, paprika, and salt to taste
1 teaspoon lemon juice
2 egg yolks, beaten
3 tablespoons sherry
Very small dash cayenne pepper

METHOD: Heat the crab meat, including the liquid from the can, in a saucepan, adding a little white pepper, paprika, salt, cayenne pepper and the lemon juice. Cover and cook until the crab meat is thoroughly warmed. When warm pour the liquid into the white sauce, stirring with a wire whip. Cooking over medium heat, slowly add the egg yolks, continuing to stir with the whip until smooth and thick. Add the crab meat, heat through, then remove from the fire, stir in the sherry, and serve immediately. Add some more paprika if you wish a sauce with a pink color.

*WHITE SAUCE—INGREDIENTS:
>2 tablespoons flour
>2 tablespoons water
>2 tablespoons butter (¼ of one stick)
>1 cup milk or ½ cup milk and ½ cup cream

METHOD: In a small saucepan, melt the butter. Mix the flour, water, and milk (or milk-cream combination) together in a cup. As soon as the butter is completely melted and begins to get hot, slowly add the flour-water-milk mixture, stirring continually. Let the sauce come to a boil for a minute, stirring constantly, then remove it from the fire. Add a few more drops of milk if you want a thinner sauce. Keep warm by placing it in a container in a hot water bath.

LIVER A LA SUISSE (p. 108)

INGREDIENTS FOR 8:
>2 pounds calves liver, or baby beef liver
>6 ounces butter (1½ sticks)
>Salt and pepper to taste
>1 tablespoon chopped parsley

4

METHOD: Remove the outside covering tissue and veins from the liver. Cut it into slices approximately ¼-inch thick. Cut the slices into 1½-inch strips. Place a large empty skillet over medium heat. When hot, add ¼ of the butter; when melted, add some of the liver, grind in some fresh black pepper, add some more butter and the remaining pieces of liver. Cover skillet with a lid and cook for 10 minutes.

Remove the lid. Add the rest of the butter, increase the heat, and with a metal spatula or spoon continue to turn the pieces of liver. After 3 or 4 minutes, add the parsley; at the last minute, just before serving, add the salt. You may prepare this dish in a chafing dish, but reduce the quantity to half, preparing for only 4 persons.

RUM OMELETTE (p. 129)

INGREDIENTS FOR 8:

- 16 fresh eggs at room temperature
- 1 cup light cream ("half & half")
- ½ teaspoon salt
- 4 ounces butter (1 stick)
- 1 cup dark rum
  Confectioners' sugar (powdered sugar)

METHOD: Beat 8 of the eggs (unless the largest frying pan or skillet that you own will not hold that many eggs, in which case, make the recipe in 3 steps using 6, then 5, and finally the last 5 eggs) with a fork until no more white or yellow shows and the consistency is rather uniformly liquified. Add ¼ teaspoon of the salt and ½ the light cream and beat again. Over medium-high heat, heat an 8- to 9-inch diameter frying pan or skillet. When it is hot, add first ¼ of the stick of butter, and coat the pan by tilting it back and forth, then add another ¼ of the stick. As soon as the butter is completely heated through, pour in the egg-cream mixture all at once. Reduce the heat to medium and gently shake and tilt the pan, loosening the edges with a spatula, and letting the remaining liquid run under the edges. As soon as the egg is set, tilt the pan away from you and carefully roll the omelette from the side closest to you to the side away from you. Turn out onto an ovenproof dish; keep warm.

Repeat the same steps with the remaining 8 eggs. Warm the rum in a small clean pot, and then pour it around the sides of the omelettes. Generously sprinkle powdered sugar through a fine sieve over the tops of the omelettes. To ignite, remove a teaspoonful of the rum and light it. Pour the flaming rum over the rest of the rum in the plate and keep spooning it over the tops of the omelettes as long as it keeps flaming. Serve immediately.

ONE HUNDRED RECIPES
FOR THE CHAFING DISH

THIS Book is intended to give pleasure to those who enjoy using a Chafing Dish. The formulas are simple, easy to follow, and are not designed to prove that elaborate dishes can be prepared, but that many articles of food can easily be made very delicate, toothsome and enjoyable.

THE CHAFING DISH.

THE Chafing Dish has played no small part in the civilization of the world. In tracing its history it is interesting to note, that it has always appeared when nations had ceased to war and had turned their attention to the science of good living and the art of enjoyment. It has ever been associated with the graces and amenities of life. Indeed, its appearance has seemed to signalize a nation's progress and to be significant of general good cheer and success.

Athenaeus, the Greek philosopher, asserted "that nothing has so powerfully contributed to instil piety into the souls of men as good cookery." That the Chafing Dish is a paramount instrument of good cookery no one will deny. That piety received an impetus from it, is easily inferred from the fact that a Chafing Dish was a familiar adjunct on the altars in old French churches. Glowing with lighted charcoal in winter it was a beacon of comfort to the faithful priests.

Its use, however, was not limited to chancels. More than two thousand years ago the Chafing Dish fulfilled its true office as the promoter of man's palatable pleasures at the tables of the wealthy Greeks and Romans. When it first appeared Seneca said of it,

"Daintiness gave birth to this useful invention in order that no viand should be chilled and that everything should be hot enough to please the most pampered palate. The kitchen follows the supper."

The Chafing Dishes of the ancient epicures were exquisite in workmanship and beautiful in design ; but it is hardly necessary to add, they were not as useful as the modern dishes.

"Each of these elegant utensils, says Soyer, who has written exhaustively of the lives and customs of the Greeks and Romans, "was supported by three geese. It measures seven inches from the extremity of one of the bird's heads to the opposite edge of the circumference. The tray is 15 lines or an inch and a quarter deep, and the feet raise it about two inches above the plane. The three geese have their wings spread and terminate by neats' feet. The heads raised on the breasts form graceful handles. These Chafing Dishes arranged systematically on the sigma produce a delightful effect."

Another writer describes a Roman banquet scene, of which the Chafing Dish was a prominent feature. "Dishes of massive silver occupy another compartment of the vast cupboard. An opulent family could not possibly do without this luxury. Sylla had some which weighed 200 marks, and Rome could produce more than 500 of the same weight. According to this enthusiastic chronicler, there was "a perfect furore for these dishes which greatly augmented in the time of the Emperor Claudius. One of his slaves named Drusillanus Rotundus possessed a silver dish weighing 1,000 marks which was served in the midst of eight smaller ones weighing 100 marks each. These nine dishes were arranged at table on a machine which supported them and placed them prominently in view"

Cicero undoubtedly referred to the Chafing Dish in making one of his most telling points in his first public law case. He was engaged to defend Sextus Roscius, who was accused of murdering his father, against Sylla, who sold the estates of Roscius for a trifling sum to his favorite slave, Chrysogonus. In making a summary of the wealth of this slave and an exposition of his luxurious living, Cicero says: "A house filled with Corinthian and Delvan vessels, among which was that celebrated stove which he so lately bought at so great a price that passers-by who heard the money being counted out, thought a farm was being sold. This was the anthepsa to which Cicero referred, and is described as "a kind of saucepan of Corinthian brass of considerable value, and made with such art that its contents cook instantly and almost without fire. This simple and ingenius vessel possessed a double bottom, the uppermost one holds the light delicacies destined for the dessert and the fire is underneath."

So popular was the Chafing Dish that a semblance of it was used for a table ornament, just as floral-pieces are used now.

Silver gridirons with Syrian plums and pomegranate seeds beneath them to simulate fire, were a feature of the table at a supper of the Roman Lentulus. Not only did the Chafing Dish adorn the tables at royal banquets and contribute to the gastronomic enjoyments of the rich, but it was in high favor then as now, among the representatives of the histrionic art. Pliny relates that the tragic actor, Aesopus, had a dish worth 1,000 sestercii. No doubt then, as at the present time, the actor enjoyed his hot midnight meal filled with grateful appreciation of the Chafing Dish, which has inspired a modern play-wright to make it the subject of an ode.

In the middle ages when strife and anarchy reigned, this utensil of polite life fell into disuse. But in the fifteenth century when learning received an impetus and the life of queen and of laymen became more elegant and comfortable, the Chafing Dish is heard of again. Lord Francis Bacon in a treatise on "Physiological Remains," used the silver Chafing Dish as a standard of comparison for durability in metals. He charges experimenters "to make proof of the incorporation of silver and tin in equal quantity, or with two parts silver and one part tin and to observe whether it will endure the ordinary fire which belongeth to Chafing Dishes, posnets and such other silver vessels."

The Chafing Dish is a cosmopolitan vessel. It belongs to all nations. It was no less appreciated by the French than the English.

But during the political turmoils and wars in France the Chafing Dish, like other comforts and enjoyments of good living, was relegated to the shelf. It might have served for the glorification of a certain minister of France, who for its lack suffered a mortification that the caustic wit of Talleyrand has immortalized. By some unfortuitous circumstance the fish when served Talleyrand was cold. "That is a magnificent carp," said the financier, "how do you like it? It came from my estate in Virsur Ainse."

"Did it?" said Talleyrand. "But why did you not have it cooked here?"

If the Chafing Dish had adorned that board, the scene might have been made as memorable for gustatory triumphs as that depicted by Philemon who gives a pleasing pen-picture of what accomplished artists, cooks were in the very olden times. 'One of the great cooks of his day, delighted at his success in using the Chafing Dish said that he cooked a fish so exquisitely that it returned him admiring and grateful looks from the frying-pan. He had treated it with such daintiness and delicacy, that, even when fully cooked, it lay on the dish as fresh looking as if it had just been taken from the lake. The result was such a rarity the delighted guests tore it from one another and a running struggle was kept up around the board to get possession of this exquisitely prepared morceau.' And yet says the cook, "I had nothing better to exhibit my talent upon than a wretched river fish, nourished in mud." This culinary boaster was so elated at his success, he declared with triumphant accents, " I think I may say that I have discovered the principle of immortality and the odors of my dishes would recall life to the nostrils of the very dead."

Although this hyperbolical assertion is highly amusing, and those who, in this practical day and generation, appreciate the epicurean delights distinctive of the Chafing Dish, would scarcely voice such an extravaganza, nevertheless feel the quickening enthusiasm that exalted this ancient cook.

The Chafing Dish ever identified with the progressive phase of life appeared in America in 1720. The colonists having overcome the difficulties incidental upon the making of a new country, began to appreciate and to desire the luxuries and adornments of refined living. The father of a rich bride of the day, who desired to give his daughter " a truly elegant outfit," in the list of household furnishings he ordered from England, included "6 small brass Chafing Dishes, 4 shillings apiece." From which fact may be inferred that the hospitable hostesses of that time were wont to give Chafing Dish parties, as do the entertainers of this enlightened century.

This period of early prosperity was followed by wars and times of such arduous toil and financial stringency that entertaining almost became a lost art.

But now that the nation prospers and life in America shows a fuller expression of beauty, refinement and artistic development, and there is time to consider the ethics of good cookery, the Chafing Dish has become as necessary a feature of the elegantly equipped modern household as it was of the luxurious homes of the ancient Greeks and Romans.

Like all beneficent things it is not for the rich alone. It ministers in more or less elegant form to all sorts and conditions of men. It is of infinite convenience to those who nurse the sick and must prepare food at irregular hours. It is a boon to the journalist who, after his nightly toil, enjoys a repast in his own home. The busy housewife whose burdens are lightened by one maid calls the Chafing Dish "the woman's friend."

The mastery of the Chafing Dish is one of the undisputed arts where a man and woman may share equal privileges and triumphs. A man may prove his skill in cooking with it without detracting from his dignity and a woman can scarcely manipulate it without adding to her charm.

The heroes of Homer prepared their repasts with their own hands and prided themselves on their culinary accomplishments. Ulysses surpassed in lighting a fire and laying a cloth; Patroclus drew wine and Achilles turned the spit. It is, therefore, not only classic, but the highest honor a host can confer upon a guest to prepare food for him with his own hands.

The Chafing Dish not only makes possible the sincerest expression of the most perfect hospitality, but it seems the true symbol of good fellowship. It develops a spirit of royal camaraderie. Even a pessimist would be inclined to judge his neighbor by his excellencies and not by his defects, as succulent odors whet the appetite and carry the sweet assurance of coming gustatory joys.

Verily, "a good dish sharpens the wit and softens the heart." Who can measure the beneficent influence of exquisite savours! The Chafing Dish is the culinary censer.

MINUTIÆ.

AN exceedingly important feature in successful Chafing Dish cooking, is that the wicks of the lamp should be perfectly trimmed, and the reservoir about one half full of alcohol, after cooking a dish, and when making preparations for another, look carefully after this feature.

Have the wicks so regulated that all available flame shall be entirely under the dish, and that none of it shall come up the sides.

As the water is very liable to boil over, it is best to have a tray under the Chafing Dish to catch it, or any other drippings.

The covers are supposed to be off the Chafing Dish in the following recipes, unless otherwise directed.

IN cooking over hot water pan, see that proper quantity of water, about one half inch, is in it.

Judgment must be used as to time; the time given in these recipes was the actual time consumed in cooking the various dishes, over full fire, with a very steady flame, and the absence of any condition (such as draughts, etc.) tending to make the flame variable.

In the recipes given, the intention has been to keep the seasoning very mild, individual tastes must be consulted as to the proper seasoning to use.

By the term "pat of butter," a piece the size of a large English walnut is intended.

A SUCCESSFUL omelette is very difficult to make in the ordinary size Chafing Dish with more than two eggs.

When using the term " cupful " in these recipes, the capacity of a full size coffee cup is intended.

See that the dish is scalded before using and thoroughly rubbed with a dry towel in order that all powder used in polishing may positively be removed.

The steel pan will be found desirable for making omelettes, frying oysters, and all dishes of this class.

An adage says " constant vigilance is the price of safety." So also is constant watchfulness a necessary element to success in the successful use of a Chafing Dish.

INDEX

INDEX

Asparagus, - - - - - - - - - 37
Bacon, - - - - - - - - - 38
Beans, Lima, - - - - - - - - 39
Beans, String, - - - - - - - - 40
Beef Steak, - - - - - - - - 43
Beef Steak and Oysters, - - - - - - 44
Beef Steak Sandwiches, - - - - - - 45
Beef Steak and Onions, - - - - - - - 46
Beef Stew, - - - - - - - - 49
Beef Stew with Curry, - - - - - - 49
Clams, Hashed, on Toast, - - - - - - 50
Crab Meat Fricassee, - - - - - - 51
Crab Meat a la Newburgh - - - - - 52
Crabs, Soft Shell, - - - - - - - 55
Chicken, Breast of, Braised, - - - - - 56
Chicken Fricassee, - - - - - - 57
Chicken Fricassee, with Curry, - - - - - 57
Chicken, Hashed, - - - - - - - 58
Chicken Legs, Deviled, - - - - - - 61
Codfish, Boiled, Parsley Sauce, - - - - - 62
Codfish in Butter, - - - - - - - 63
Codfish, Salt, in Cream, - - - - - - 64
Corned Beef Hash, - - - - - - - 67

INDEX.

Corn, Sweet, - - - - - - - - - 68

Deviled Sauce, - . - - - - - 69

Duck Legs, Deviled, - - - - - - - 70

Duck, Breast of Wild, Braised, - - - - - 71

Duck, Breast of Tame, Braised, - - - - 72

Eggs, Boiled, - - - - - - - 75

Eggs, en Casserole, - - - - - - 76

Eggs, Scrambled, , - - - - - - 77

Eggs, Scrambled, with Tomatoes, - - - - 78

Eggs, Scrambled, with Asparagus Points, - - - 78

Eggs, Scrambled, with Sausages, - - - - 81

Eggs, Scrambled, with Bacon, - - - - 82

Eggs, Scrambled, with Ham, - - - - 83

Eggs, Scrambled, with Artichoke Hearts, - - - 84

Eggs, Scrambled, with Mushrooms, - - - - 87

Frogs Legs in Butter, - - - - - - 88

Frogs Legs Fricassee, - - - - - 89

Frogs Legs a la Newburgh, - - - - - 89

Grouse, Breast of, Braised, - - - - 90

Halibut, Boiled, - - - - - - - 93

Halibut, Boiled, Egg Sauce, - - - - - 94

Ham Braised, - - - - - - - 95

Jamieson Scramble, - - - - - - 96

INDEX

Jowl, Smoked Pigs, and Hominy, 97
Kidney, Deviled, 98
Lamb Chops, 101
Lamb Cutlets. 102
Lamb Hash, 103
Lamb Stew, 104
Lamb Stew with Curry 104
Lamb, Deviled, 107
Liver a la Suisse, 108
Liver and Bacon, 109
Lobster Fricassee, 110
Lobster a la Newburgh, 110
Lobster in Butter, 113
Lobster, Deviled, 114
Mutton Chops, 115
Mutton Cutlets, 116
Mutton Hash, 117
Mutton, Deviled, 118
Mutton Stew, 121
Mutton, with Curry and Rice, 122
Mushrooms, Braised, 123
Omelette, Plain, 124
Omelette with Parsley, 124

INDEX

Omelette with Bacon,   - . . - . 127
Omelette with Jelly, - - . . 128
Omelette with Rum,   - . . - 129
Onions in Cream,   - . . - - 130
Onions Braised,   - . . - . 131
Oysters, Fried,   . - . . - 132
Oysters, Roasted, - - - . - 135
Oysters, Stewed in Milk, - - . - 136
Oysters Fricassee, - - . . - 137
Oysters a la Newburgh,   - - . 137
Oyster Crabs in Butter, - . - - 138
Oyster Crabs Fricassee,   - . . 141
Oyster Crabs a la Newburgh,   - . - 141
Partridge, Breast of, Braised, - . 142
Pan Cakes,   - . . - . 143
Peas, French,   . - . . - . 144
Pepper Pot, - . - . - . 147
Pigs Feet in Butter, - . . 148
Potatoes, Boiled, - . . - 149
Potatoes, Stewed in Cream,   - . . 150
Potatoes, Sweet, - . . - . 151
Quail, Breast of, Braised, - . . - 152
Reed Birds, ... - . 155

31

Roast Beef Hash,   -   -   -   -   -   156
Roast Beef, Deviled,   -   -   -   -   -   157
Sausage, Frankfurter, and Cabbage -   -   -   158
Smelts in Butter,   -   -   -   -   -   161
Sweetbreads, Braised,   -   -   -   162
Squabs, Braised,   -   -   -   -   -   163
Succotash,   -   -   -   -   -   -   164
Tripe with Onions, -   -   -   -   -   167
Tripe with Tomatoes,   -   -   -   -   168
Turkey, Breast of, Braised,   -   -   -   169
Turkey Stew,   -   -   -   -   -   170
Turkey with Curry,   -   -   -   -   170
Turkey, Hash, -   -   -   -   -   171
Turkey Legs, Deviled,   -   -   -   -   172
Veal Cutlets in Butter,   -   -   -   -   175
Veal, Deviled,   -   -   -   -   -   176
Venison Steak,   -   -   -   -   -   177
Venison Steak, Currant Jelly Sauce.   -   -   177
Welsh Rarebit,   -   -   -   -   -   178
White Fish, Boiled,   -   -   -   -   181
White Sauce,   -   -   -   -   -   182

Recipes

Asparagus.

PUT the tender part of two dozen stocks of asparagus in hot water and boil for fifteen minutes, adding a little salt. Drain, season to taste and serve, either with white sauce made as per recipe, or plain butter. If canned asparagus is used, put plenty of cold water into the can and let it drain off thoroughly ; put asparagus with a little salt into the hot water and let it remain until thoroughly heated through, when drain on a napkin, and serve with white sauce or butter.

Bacon.

PLACE eight slices in Chafing Dish over open fire and when it begins to cook turn it ; continuing to do so until it is thoroughly cooked through, being careful not to burn.

Lima Beans.

MELT two large pats of butter in Chafing Dish, put in one can of Lima beans, first washed in cold water and drained. Cook over open fire until beans are thoroughly hot. Season to taste and serve.

String Beans.

MELT two large pats of butter in Chafing Dish, put in one can of string beans, first washed in cold water and drained. Cook over open fire until they are thoroughly hot. Season to taste and serve.

As string beans are not quite so delicate as Lima beans, they will take a little longer to cook.

PLATED CHAFING DISH No. 0495.

CAPACITY FOUR HALF PINTS.

MADE BY GORHAM MFG. CO.

Consisting of
Chafing Dish and Cover
Stand and Lamp
Hot Water Pan
Cutlet Dish

Form round
Finish, Satin or Polished
Handle, Ebony

Plain Beefsteak.

PUT pat of butter in Chafing Dish and let thoroughly melt ; have nice rump or sirloin steak, one pound in two pieces, about one inch thick prepared by being nicely trimmed, put in dish ; cook on one side for ten minutes, turn and cook for five minutes over hot water, cover on. Season to taste. Can be served plain or with a little chopped parsley. A little paprika makes a delicious seasoning.

Beefsteak with Oysters.

COOK the steak as per recipe for plain beefsteak, page 43, put it on a hot platter, cook twenty large oysters, as per recipe, page 135. Pour them over the steak and serve.

Flank, Rump or Sirloin Steak Sandwiches.

ONE pound of steak one inch thick; melt three pats of butter, put in the steak and cook about six minutes; turn it on the other side and cook about four minutes when it will be finished. Have ready some thin slices of Graham or white bread, each slice cut in two pieces; with a very sharp knife, carve the steak crosswise in thin slices, lay upon the half cut of bread, season with pepper, salt and paprika, put on this a little of the gravy, and then the other half slice of bread. Do not use knife and fork, but eat as you would a sandwich.

Beefsteak and Onions.

PUT two pats of butter in Chafing Dish and let it become thoroughly hot. Cut one pound of beef-steak, about one half inch thick, into slices and cook in the butter about five minutes, when put in three tablespoonfuls of chopped onions and cook five minutes more. Sprinkle with salt and pepper and add three tablespoonfuls of bouillon and a little chopped parsley.

PLATED CHAFING DISH No. 0520.

CAPACITY FIVE HALF PINTS.

MADE BY GORHAM MFG. CO.

Consisting of
Chafing Dish and Cover
Stand and Lamp
Hot Water Pan
Cutlet Dish

Form, oval
Finish, satin or polished

Beef Stew.

MAKE white sauce as per recipe ; put in one pound of cold roast beef, cut into large dice pieces, and four medium sized cold boiled potatoes, sliced.

When meat and potatoes are thoroughly warmed through, season to taste and serve. A little chopped parsley or shives may be added if desired.

To make beef stew with curry, add heaping teaspoonful of curry powder to above.

Hashed Little Neck Clams on Toast.

MELT pat of butter in Chafing Dish, then put in three dozen Little Neck clams, hashed fine, and their juice, add a teaspoonful of chopped shives and two of parsley. Cook over open fire until it boils up twice, cover on, thicken with bread crumbs, add two tablespoonfuls of Sherry, season to taste and serve on butter toast.

Crab Meat Fricassee.

MAKE white sauce in Chafing Dish as per recipe, put in two cupfuls of crab meat, add a little pepper, paprika, a teaspoonful of vinegar or lemon juice, and a trifle of Cayenne. Mix thoroughly with sauce. Cook until meat is thoroughly warmed through, being careful not to burn. Season to taste and serve.

Crab Meat a la Newburgh.

MAKE white sauce, as per recipe, put in Chafing Dish with two cupfuls of crab meat, adding a little pepper, paprika, a teaspoonful of vinegar or lemon juice, and a dash of Cayenne. Cook until meat is thoroughly warmed through, then add three tablespoonfuls of Sherry, and the yolk of two eggs whipped —don't let boil after eggs go in. Season to taste and serve.

PLATED CHAFING DISH No. 0526.

CAPACITY THREE HALF PINTS.

MADE BY GORHAM MFG. CO.

Consisting of
Chafing Dish and Cover
Stand and Lamp
Hot Water Pan

Form, round
Finish, bright
Handle, ebony

Soft Shell Crabs.

PUT four pats of butter into the Chafing Dish, and let it become very hot, then put in four medium sized soft shell crabs, first prepared by removing the lungs and washing thoroughly, add two teaspoonfuls of lemon juice. Cook about ten minutes, being careful they do not burn. Season with a little salt and white pepper. Serve on toast or plain.

Breast of Chicken Braised.

MELT four pats of butter in Chafing Dish and let become thoroughly hot, put in with the butter the breasts of two chickens in four pieces, first taking off the skin. Cook over open fire for six minutes, turn and cook five minutes, being careful not to burn. Season to taste and serve.

Fricassee of Chicken.

MAKE white sauce in Chafing Dish, as per recipe, add the white and dark meat of a cold boiled chicken weighing from three to four pounds, cut into large dice pieces. Season with pepper and salt and cook over open fire until meat is thoroughly warmed, being careful not to burn.

If sauce should cook too thick, thin with boiled milk or cream.

To make Fricassee with curry, add an even teaspoonful of curry powder.

Chicken Hash.

PUT in Chafing Dish four pats of butter and let thoroughly melt, mix one pound of finely chopped cold roast or boiled chicken and an equal quantity in bulk of finely chopped cold boiled potatoes moistened with one half a cup of bouillon. Put in dish and cook over open fire until chicken and potatoes are well warmed through, being careful not to burn. Season to taste. Sprinkle with a tablespoonful of finely chopped parsley and serve.

PLATED CHAFING DISH, No. 0560.

CAPACITY FOUR HALF PINTS.

MADE BY GORHAM MFG. CO.

Consisting of
Chafing Dish and Cover
Stand and Lamp
Hot Water Pan
 Cutlet Dish, if wanted

Form, round.
Finish, polished
Handles ivory

Legs of Chicken Deviled.

MAKE deviled sauce in Chafing Dish, as per recipe, put in uncooked second joints and drum sticks of two chickens, boned. Cook over hot water pan for ten minutes and finish over open fire for ten minutes, cover on, being careful not to burn.

If cold roast or boiled chicken are to be used, cook five minutes or until thoroughly heated through.

Fresh Codfish Boiled.

PUT in the Chafing Dish about one and one half pints of hot water, and when it comes to a boil, add two teaspoonfuls of vinegar or lemon juice, put in one and one half pounds of codfish, cut lengthwise, bone out fish, and cook over open fire with cover on, for twelve minutes. Put on plate, season to taste and serve.

Chopped parsley mixed with melted butter makes a nice dressing.

Fresh Codfish in Butter.

PUT in the Chafing Dish three pats of butter and let become thoroughly heated, then put in one and one half pounds fresh codfish, cut lengthwise, bone out, sprinkle a little salt over the top, add a teaspoonful of lemon juice or vinegar. Cook for nine minutes over open fire, turn and cook for six minutes, being careful not to let it stick to the pan; add about one teaspoonful each of chopped shives and parsley in sauce. Season to taste and serve.

Salt Codfish with Cream.

MELT three pats of butter in Chafing Dish, put in two heaping teaspoonfuls of flour and one cupful or sufficient cream to make proper consistency, constantly stir to keep sauce smooth, then add two cupfuls of picked and freshened codfish. Cook for twelve minutes over hot water, cover on ; put in a beaten up egg, season to taste, and serve on buttered toast, or with baked potatoes.

PLATED CHAFING DISH No. 0560.

CAPACITY FOUR HALF PINTS.

MADE BY GORHAM MFG. CO.

Consisting of
Chafing Dish and Cover
Stand and Lamp
Hot Water Pan
(Cutlet Dish, if wanted)

Form, round
Finish, repousse chased
Handles, ivory

Corned Beef Hash.

MELT two pats of butter in the Chafing Dish and cook with it a tablespoonful of chopped celery; prepare hash by chopping fine in a chopping bowl, three-quarters of a pound of cold boiled brisket or plate corned beef, not too fat, and an equal quantity of freshly boiled potatoes, moisten it with two thirds of a cup of bouillon or beef stock. Mix thoroughly and cook over open fire for fifteen minutes, being careful not to burn. Season to taste and serve.

A pinch of chopped shives, onions or shallots can be added if desired, but if used, they should be cooked with the butter and celery.

Sweet Corn.

MELT two large pats of butter in Chafing Dish, then put in one can of sweet corn; do not wash the corn. Cook over open fire until corn is thoroughly hot. Season with salt and pepper and serve.

Deviled Sauce.

PUT in Chafing Dish, over open fire, two pats of butter, two teaspoonfuls of chopped parsley, one of mixed English mustard, two chopped onions, and two tablespoonfuls of vinegar; after butter is well melted cook two minutes, keep continually stirring; add one tablespoonful of Worcestershire sauce, a good pinch of salt, some black pepper and a little cayenne.

Additional mustard and Worcestershire sauce may be added if desired to have it more sharp.

Legs of Tame Duck Deviled.

MAKE deviled sauce in Chafing Dish, as per recipe, put in uncooked second joints and drum sticks of two tame ducks, boned ; cook over hot water pan for ten minutes and finish over open fire for ten minutes, cover on, being careful not to burn.

If cold roast or boiled tame duck are to be used, cook five minutes or until thoroughly heated through.

Breast of Wild Duck Braised.

MELT four pats of butter in Chafing Dish, and let it become thoroughly hot ; prepare two breasts, by removing the skin and cutting into four pieces ; put them in with the butter and cook over open fire for five minutes and four minutes after turning. Be careful not to burn. Season to taste. When about done, add two teaspoonfuls of jelly ; or, instead of cooking with the jelly, can serve with it, if preferred.

Breast of Tame Duck Braised.

MELT four pats of butter in Chafing Dish and let become thoroughly hot, put the breasts of two ducks, in four pieces, skin off, in with the butter and cook over open fire for six minutes; turn and cook five minutes. Be careful not to burn. Season to taste and serve.

PLATED CHAFING DISH No. 0565.

CAPACITY THREE HALF PINTS.

MADE BY GORHAM MFG, CO.

Consisting of
Chafing Dish and Cover
Stand and Lamp
Hot Water Pan
(Cutlet Dish, if wanted)

Form, round
Finish, polished
Handles, ivory

Boiled Eggs.

A S soon as water comes to a boil, put in eggs. Raise up side of pan occasionally, thus moving the eggs and insuring a uniform cooking. Cover and cook three minutes.

Another way :

Have water boiling hot, put in the eggs, and after one minute, put out the lamp and leave the eggs in five minutes, cover on.

Eggs en Casserole.

PUT a cup into the boiling water; after it is thoroughly heated break two eggs into it, put cover on, and cook four minutes. Flavor to taste with salt and pepper.

This is the most delicate way of cooking an egg, and for invalids is especially recommended.

Scrambled Eggs.

MELT three pats of butter in Chafing Dish; when thoroughly hot, put in eight eggs, well beaten, four tablespoonfuls of cream and a teaspoonful of salt well mixed. When cooked to proper consistency, scramble, turn on platter and serve.

Scrambled Eggs with Tomatoes.

MELT three pats of butter in Chafing Dish and when thoroughly hot put in eight eggs, well beaten, with four tablespoonfuls of cream and a teaspoonful of salt, well mixed ; when eggs commence to scramble, put in six tablespoonfuls of the dry part of canned tomatoes, and cook to the proper consistency. Season to taste and serve.

Asparagus points may be treated same as tomatoes.

PLATED CHAFING DISH No. 0570.

CAPACITY FIVE HALF PINTS.

MADE BY GORHAM MFG. CO.

Consisting of
Chafing Dish and Cover
Stand and Lamp
Hot Water Pan
(Cutlet Dish, if wanted)

Form, oval
Finish, polished
Handles, ivory

Scrambled Eggs and Sausage.

PUT six links of sausage, after taking off the casings, in Chafing Dish and cook thoroughly over open fire ; cut up into small pieces, pour off half of the fat and add two pats of butter, eight raw eggs, well beaten, in a bowl with four tablespoonfuls of cream. Mix with the sausage and cook until proper consistency, Season to taste and serve.

Scrambled Eggs and Bacon.

CUT into pieces one-half an inch long eight thin slices of bacon, put in Chafing Dish and cook over open fire until not too well done; if bacon is very rich, pour off some of the fat; then put in dish eight eggs, well beaten, with four tablespoonfuls of cream. Cook to proper consistency, serve plain or on toast or Graham bread sliced thin.

Scrambled Eggs and Ham.

CUT one slice of cold boiled ham into pieces about one inch square and put in Chafing Dish with one pat of butter. Cook over open fire until ham is well warmed through, when add eight eggs, well beaten, with four tablespoonfuls of cream. Cook to proper consistency, and serve.

Scrambled Eggs with Artichoke Hearts.

PUT three pats of butter in Chafing Dish and let become thoroughly melted, then add four canned artichoke hearts, cut into dice pieces; when heated through put in eight eggs, well beaten, with four tablespoonfuls of cream. Cook over open fire until proper consistency. Season to taste, and serve.

PLATED YACHT CHAFING DISH No. 0619.

CAPACITY FOUR HALF PINTS.

MADE BY GORHAM MFG. CO.

Consisting of
Chafing Dish and Cover
Stand and Lamp
Hot Water Pan

Form, round
Finish, polished
Handle, ebony

Scrambled Eggs with Mushrooms.

PUT two pats of butter in Chafing Dish, let it become thoroughly hot, then put in one-half can of mushrooms, cut into slices; when warmed through add eight eggs, well beaten, with four tablespoonfuls of cream. Cook over open fire to proper consistency. Season to taste and serve.

A tablespoonful of sherry can be added to the dish before putting in the eggs, if desired.

Frogs' Legs in Butter.

PUT four pats of butter in Chafing Dish and let it become thoroughly melted, add a little salt, two teaspoonfuls of lemon juice or vinegar, one and one-half dozen of medium-sized mushrooms, skinned and sliced thin, and three dozen medium-sized frogs' legs. Cook over open fire about fifteen minutes, may be covered part of the time, being careful not to burn. Sprinkle with chopped parsley and serve.

Frogs' Legs Fricassee

PUT three pats of butter in Chafing Dish and let become thoroughly melted, add a little salt and two teaspoonfuls of lemon juice or vinegar; put in three dozen medium sized frogs' legs; cover dish and cook for thirteen minutes over open fire, being careful not to burn; remove the juice, add one and one-half cupfuls of white sauce. If too thick, thin with some of the juice removed. Cook about three minutes, season to taste and serve.

To make Newburgh, add three tablespoonfuls of sherry and the yolks of two eggs, well beaten.

Breast of Grouse Braised.

MELT four pats of butter in Chafing Dish and let become thoroughly hot; put the breasts of two grouse, in four pieces, skin off, in with the butter and cook over open fire for six minutes; turn and cook five minutes. Be careful not to burn. Season to taste and serve.

PLATED CHAFING DISH No. 0620.

CAPACITY FIVE HALF PINTS.

MADE BY GORHAM MFG. CO.

Consisting of
Chafing Dish and Cover
Stand and Lamp
Hot Water Pan

Form, round
Finish, polished
Handles, ebony

Chicken Halibut.

PUT in the Chafing Dish three pats of butter and let become thoroughly heated, then put in one and one half pounds of fresh chicken halibut, cut lengthwise, bone out ; sprinkle a little salt over the top, add a teaspoonful of lemon juice or vinegar. Cook for nine minutes over open fire ; turn and cook for six minutes, being careful not to let it stick to the pan ; add about one teaspoonful each of chopped shives and parsley in sauce. Season to taste and serve.

Egg Sauce.

MIX in a bowl, three heaping teaspoonfuls of flour with a pat of butter, add a little water, and thin with milk or cream ; put in Chafing Dish over hot water pan ; salt to taste ; keep continually stirring until thoroughly cooked.   As it thickens add milk or cream, until the proper consistency, when done let it come to a boil for an instant, being careful not to burn ; add three hard boiled eggs, cut into small dice pieces.

Braised Ham.

PUT in Chafing Dish one pat of butter, let it get thoroughly hot, when add four thin slices of ham, using only the tender part. Cook over open fire about four minutes, turn and cook three minutes. Be careful that ham does not burn or become too dry. Season with a little pepper, if desired, and serve.

Jamieson Scramble.

ONE half cupful of flour, one even teaspoonful of salt, same of white pepper, one half teaspoonful of paprika ; one teaspoonful of baking powder, two eggs, well beaten ; make into a batter with milk or cream ; add one cupful of raw veal, chopped fine, mix all thoroughly together. Make hot in Chafing Dish one pat of butter and put in thin layer of the mixture. Cook over open fire until light brown on the under side, then turn and brown the other side. Be careful it does not adhere to the pan. The above will make four scrambles.

Smoked Pigs Jowl.

MELT two pats of butter in Chafing Dish and let it become hot. Prepare four slices of boiled smoked jowl by sprinkling it freely with powdered sugar on both sides. Put it in the butter and cook over open fire, on both sides, till heated thoroughly. Serve with Boston brown or Graham bread, cut thin.

Lambs' Kidney, Deviled.

MAKE deviled sauce in Chafing Dish, as per recipe.
Prepare eight kidneys by cutting them lengthwise so that they will lay open flat. Salt the cut side ;
put in with the sauce and cook over open fire, cut side
down, three minutes, turn and cook seven minutes.
Garnish with sauce in which kidneys are cooked.

PLATED CHAFING DISH No. 0625.

CAPACITY THREE HALF PINTS.

MADE BY GORHAM MFG. CO.

Consisting of
Chafing Dish and Cover
Stand and Lamp
Hot Water Pan

Form, round
Finish, polished
Handles, ebony

Lamb Chops.

PUT two pats of butter in Chafing Dish, melt thoroughly, then put in eight trimmed lamb chops without the bone. Cook over hot water pan, cover on, for six minutes, turn and cook four minutes. Season to taste and serve.

Lamb Cutlets, from Leg.

PUT two pats of butter in Chafing Dish and let it become thoroughly melted, then put in two lamb cutlets; cook over hot water, cover on, for eight minutes, turn and cook four minutes. Season to taste and serve.

Lamb Hash.

PUT in Chafing Dish four pats of butter and melt thoroughly. Mix one pound of finely chopped cold roast lamb and an equal quantity in bulk of finely chopped, cold, boiled potatoes, moistened with one-half cup of bouillon, put in dish and cook over open fire until meat and potatoes are well warmed through. Season to taste. Sprinkle with a tablespoonful of finely chopped parsley and serve. A tablespoonful of chopped shives or onions can be added if desired, but should be first cooked with the butter.

Lamb Stew.

MAKE white sauce as per recipe. Put in one pound of cold roast lamb, cut into dice pieces, and four medium sized, sliced, cold boiled potatoes. When meat and potatoes are thoroughly warmed through, season to taste and serve. A little chopped parsley or shives may be added if desired.

To make lamb stew with curry, add heaping tea-spoonful of curry powder to above.

PLATED CHAFING DISH, No. 01000.

CAPACITY FIVE HALF PINTS.

MADE BY GORHAM MFG. CO.

Consisting of
Chafing Dish and Cover
Stand and Lamp
Hot Water Pan
(Cutlet Dish, if wanted)

Form, oval
Finish, polished
Handles, ebony

Lamb Deviled.

MAKE deviled sauce in Chafing Dish as per recipe. Put in two cupfuls of cold roast lamb, cut in pieces about one inch square and one-half inch thick. Cook over open fire until meat is heated through, being careful not to burn. Should sauce not be "hot" enough, add seasoning to taste.

Liver a la Suisse.

PUT four pats of butter in Chafing Dish, let it become thoroughly melted and hot. Prepare one pound of liver by skinning it, and cutting into slices size of lead pencil, and one inch long. Cook over hot water for ten minutes, cover on ; then over open fire, stirring constantly, about five minutes, until it is cooked through, but not dried out. Season to taste, with pepper, salt and chopped parsley, and serve.

This with boiled or baked potatoes is a delicious breakfast or luncheon dish.

Calf's Liver and Bacon.

COOK rare eight thin slices of bacon in Chafing Dish, over open fire ; take the bacon out leaving fat in dish, put on plate and keep warm ; put in eight medium slices of liver and cook five minutes, turn it over, put in bacon, and finish. Add two pats of butter, salt and pepper to taste and serve.

Lobster Fricassee.

MAKE white sauce as per recipe and put in Chafing Dish with the meat of two two-pound lobsters cut into medium small pieces, cook over open fire until lobster is well warmed through. Season to taste and serve.

To make Lobster a la Newburgh, add three table-spoonfuls of sherry and the yolks of two eggs, well beaten.

PLATED CHAFING DISH, No. 01005.

CAPACITY FOUR HALF PINTS.

MADE BY GORHAM MFG. CO.

Consisting of
Chafing Dish and Cover
Stand and Lamp
Hot Water Pan
(Cutlet Dish, if wanted)

Form, round
Finish, polished
Handles, ebony

Lobster in Butter.

PUT four pats of butter in Chafing Dish and let become entirely melted. Then put in meat of two two-pound lobsters, cut into pieces not too small, two teaspoonfuls of lemon juice, a little salt and white pepper. Cook over open fire in the butter until lobster is thoroughly heated through. Sprinkle with finely chopped parsley and serve.

Lobster Deviled.

MAKE deviled sauce in Chafing Dish as per recipe, cut up the meat of two two-pound lobsters into medium pieces, put in the dish with the sauce, and cook over open fire about three minutes, or until lobster is heated through. If not enough seasoning, add to taste.

Mutton Chops.

PUT two pats of butter in Chafing Dish, melt thoroughly, then put in four trimmed rib chops, without the bone. Chops should be three-quarters of an inch thick. Cook over hot water pan, cover on, for eight minutes, turn and cook five minutes. Season to taste and serve.

Mutton Cutlets from Leg.

PUT three pats of butter in Chafing Dish, melt thoroughly, then put in two cutlets; cutlets should be about three-quarters of an inch thick. Cook over hot water pan, cover on, for ten minutes, turn and cook five minutes. Season to taste and serve.

Mutton Hash.

PUT in Chafing Dish four pats of butter and let melt.

Mix one pound of finely chopped cold roast mutton and an equal quantity in bulk of finely chopped cold boiled potatoes, moistened with one-half cup of bouillon; put in dish and cook over open fire until meat and potatoes are well warmed through. Season to taste, sprinkle with a tablespoonful of finely chopped parsley, and serve.

Mutton Deviled.

MAKE deviled sauce in Chafing Dish as per recipe. Put in two cupfuls of cold roast mutton, cut in pieces about one inch square and one-half inch thick. Cook over open fire until meat is heated through, being careful not to burn. Should sauce not be "hot" enough, add seasoning to taste.

PLATED CHAFING DISH. No. 01010.

CAPACITY THREE HALF PINTS.

MADE BY GORHAM MFG. CO.

Consisting of
Chafing Dish and Cover
Stand and Lamp
Hot Water Pan
(Cutlet Dish, if wanted)

Form, round
Finish, polished
Handles, ebony

Mutton Stew.

MAKE white sauce as per recipe ; put in one pound of cold roast or boiled mutton, cut into dice pieces, and four medium sized sliced cold boiled potatoes. When meat and potatoes are thoroughly warmed through, season to taste and serve. A little chopped parsley or shives may be added if desired.

To make mutton stew with curry, add heaping teaspoonful of curry powder.

Curry of Mutton and Rice.

PUT in Chafing Dish, over hot water, two cupfuls of mutton broth and three teaspoonfuls of browned flour, salt to taste; add an even tablespoonful of curry. When thoroughly hot, put in cupful of boiled rice and two cupfuls of cut up cold mutton (not too small pieces), put on cover and cook until meat and rice are warmed through, then serve.

Roast mutton can be used with butter and water and cream or milk, but it is better if made with boiled mutton and the broth.

Mushrooms Braised.

MELT in Chafing Dish, over open fire, three pats of butter, when it becomes hot put in, top down, thirty medium sized mushrooms, washed and peeled. Cook fifteen minutes, being careful the butter does not burn. Season with salt and pepper and pour over them the juice they were cooked in, and sprinkle with chopped parsley. Serve plain or on toast.

Omelette.

PUT pat of butter in Chafing Dish, over open fire and let it become hot, then pour in dish two eggs, well beaten, with two tablespoonfuls of cream and a little salt. As soon as it begins to thicken around the edges lift them carefully, allowing the melted butter to run under the cooking omelette. When to the proper consistency roll carefully with a pan cake turner and serve on a hot platter.

If desired, finely chopped parsley or shives can be sprinkled over omelette before rolling.

CHAFING DISH SPOONS

MADE BY GORHAM MFG. CO.

No. 025 ivory handle
      plated bowl
" 020 ebony handle
      plated bowl
" 015 ivory handle
      plated bowl
" 010 ebony handle
      plated bowl

No. 810 ivory handle
      sterling silver bowl
" 809 ivory handle
      sterling silver bowl

Illustrations about ½ size.

Omelette with Bacon.

CUT eight thin slices of bacon in pieces one-half inch long and put in Chafing Dish, over open fire. Cook carefully without burning. When done, take the bacon out of the dish and drain off the fat. Then put in dish one pat of butter. When butter is melted put in two eggs, well beaten, with two tablespoonfuls of cream and a little salt. When omelette is ready to be rolled, lay in the centre one-quarter of the bacon, then roll and serve. Place the remainder of the bacon on side of dish.

Omelette with Jelly.

PUT pat of butter in Chafing Dish over open fire and let it become hot, then pour in dish two eggs, well beaten, with two tablespoonfuls of cream and a little salt. As soon as it begins to thicken around the edges, lift them carefully allowing the melted butter to run under the cooking omelette. When to the proper consistency spread thinly and evenly with jelly, roll carefully and serve.

Rum Omelette.

PUT in Chafing Dish, over open fire, a pat of butter; as soon as it is bubbling hot put in two eggs, well beaten, with two tablespoonfuls of cream and a little salt; cook until it will not run in the pan, then roll, put on platter, sprinkle freely on top with powdered sugar, pour on the sides plenty of rum, set on fire, and with a spoon pour the burning liquor over the top as long as it will blaze.

Onions in Cream.

WASH, peel and cut, medium fine, four good-sized onions; put into Chafing Dish with enough cold water to cover them ; add a little salt and boil over open fire for twenty minutes, or until onions are tender. Drain off the water, add cream sufficient to cover the onions, let come to a boil, add two pats of butter, melt, mix and serve.   Season to taste.

Can be served plain or on buttered toast.

Onions Braised.

PUT in Chafing Dish two pats of butter, when melted and hot add four good sized onions, peeled and
cut into strips ; cook over open fire twelve minutes,
or until onions are tender ; be careful not to burn.
Season to taste and serve.

Fried Oysters.

MELT six pats of butter in Chafing Dish and when it is as hot as possible put in twenty-four large oysters prepared as follows : Dry the oysters in a napkin, then mix some flour and milk (or water) to a very thin and smooth batter, dip the oysters in this batter, take them out and turn them in fresh bread crumbs. Cook over open fire until well browned, drain off the butter and let oysters dry a little before serving.

STERLING SILVER CHAFING DISH $\frac{925}{1000}$ FINE. No. 5.

CAPACITY THREE HALF PINTS.

MADE BY GORHAM MFG. CO.

Consisting of
Chafing Dish and Cover
Stand and Lamp
Hot Water Pan

Form, round
Finish, polished
Handles, ivory

Roast Oysters.

PUT juice of twenty-four large oysters in Chafing Dish over open fire, let it come to a boil, when skim off the froth, then add two pats of butter and the oysters. When oysters are shrivelled, season to taste and serve—plain or on toast.

Oysters Stewed in Milk.

PUT the broth of twenty-four large oysters in Chafing Dish over hot water and let come to a boil, then skim off the froth and put into a bowl; keep warm if possible. Put pint of milk in Chafing Dish and let it come to a boil, then add two pats of butter, the broth of the oysters and the oysters. Cook until oysters become shrivelled, season with pepper and a little salt and serve.

Fricassee of Oysters,

PUT the broth of twenty-four large oysters into the Chafing Dish and let it come to a boil, then skim off the froth, put in the oysters and two pats of butter, and cook over hot water until oysters are shrivelled; add two cupfuls of white sauce, mix, season to taste and serve.

To make Oysters a la Newburgh, add three table-spoonfuls of sherry and the yolks of two eggs, well beaten.

Oyster Crabs in Butter.

PUT three pats of butter in Chafing Dish, thoroughly
melt, and when hot, put in one and one-half cupfuls of crabs, stir and cook over open fire about five
minutes, or until they become bright pink; add a
tablespoonful of lemon juice, or a pony glass of white
wine. Season with a little pepper and salt and serve
at once, either plain or on toast, or in patty crusts.

STERLING SILVER CHAFING DISH 1000 FINE. No. 10.

CAPACITY FOUR HALF PINTS.

MADE BY GORHAM MFG. CO.

Consisting of
Chafing Dish and Cover
Stand and Lamp
Hot Water Pan
(Cutlet Dish to order)

Form, round
Finish, polished
Handles, ivory

Oyster Crabs Fricassee.

PUT two cupfuls of white sauce, made as per recipe, into Chafing Dish, over hot water, and one and one half cupfuls of oyster crabs; first prepared as per recipe for oyster crabs in butter. Serve on Graham or white bread toast.

To make oyster crabs a la Newburgh, add three tablespoonfuls of sherry and the yolk of one egg, well beaten.

Breast of Partridge Braised.

MELT four pats of butter in Chafing Dish and let become hot; put the breast of two partridges, in four pieces, skin off, in with the butter and cook over open fire for six minutes; turn and cook five minutes. Be careful not to burn. Season to taste and serve.

Pancakes.

BEAT the yolks and whites of three eggs separately, then together ; add one cup of milk, one half teaspoonful of salt, one teaspoonful of fine sugar, one-half cupful of flour; mix thoroughly till smooth. Melt small pat of butter in Chafing Dish, over open fire, and when hot pour into the pan a thin layer of the mixture. When it is browned a little on the under side, turn it over with a palette knife or cake turner and brown the other side. Put it on a plate, sprinkle with fine sugar or jelly, make into a roll, and serve. This mixture will make six pancakes.

French Peas.

MELT two large pats of butter in Chafing Dish, put in one can of peas, first washed in cold water and drained. Cook over open fire until peas are thoroughly hot. Season to taste and serve.

STERLING SILVER CHAFING DISH 925/1000 FINE. No. 15.

CAPACITY FOUR HALF PINTS.

MADE BY GORHAM MFG. CO.

Consisting of
Chafing Dish and Cover
Stand and Lamp
Hot Water Pan
(Cutlet Dish to order)

Form, round
Finish, polished
Handles, ivory

Pepper Pot.

MELT four pats of butter; add and cook until soft two heaping tablespoonfuls of chopped onions, then add one tablespoonful of flour; when this is cooked, pour in two cupfuls of bouillon, the meat of one cold boiled chicken cut in large dice pieces, same quantity of honeycomb tripe, and same of cold boiled potatoes, one-half can of mushrooms sliced, six leaves of dried tabasco, or one-quarter teaspoonful of cayenne pepper. Let the mixture become thoroughly heated through. Season with one-half teaspoonful of paprika, one-third teaspoonful of black or white pepper, a proper quantity of salt, and two heaping tablespoonfuls chopped parsley. Mix and serve.

Pigs Feet.

THOROUGHLY melt two pats of butter in Chafing Dish over hot water, split two feet lengthwise into four pieces and put in the dish. Cook under cover for ten minutes, turn and cook for five minutes. Season to taste and serve. This recipe is for feet that have been previously prepared by your butcher.

Three parts tomato catsup and one part horse radish, not heated, makes a very nice sauce.

Boiled Potatoes.

PUT four good sized potatoes, sliced thin, in Chafing Dish, cover with boiling water and add one-half teaspoonful of salt; let them boil for twenty minutes over open fire, cover on, being careful that the potatoes do not stick to the bottom of the pan. Drain off the water, put potatoes on a plate, add butter and salt to taste and serve.

Potatoes Stewed in Cream.

PUT about a pint of boiling water in Chafing Dish and a heaping teaspoonful of salt. Add four good sized potatoes sliced thin, or cut lengthwise, and boil for fifteen minutes, cover on. Be careful the potatoes do not stick to bottom of dish. Drain off the water and add two cupfuls of white sauce or plain cream, let come to a boil, when season to taste and serve.

Sweet Potatoes.

MELT four pats of butter in Chafing Dish and let become hot, then put in four good sized, cold boiled, sweet potatoes, sliced thin. Cook and toss about ten minutes over open fire, being careful not to burn. Salt to taste and serve.

Breast of Quail Braised.

MELT four pats of butter in Chafing Dish and let
become thoroughly hot, put the breasts of two
quails, in four pieces, in with the butter, and cook
over open fire for six minutes ; turn and cook five
minutes. Be careful not to burn. Season to taste
and serve.

STERLING SILVER CHAFING DISH 925 FINE, No. 20.

CAPACITY THREE HALF PINTS.

MADE BY GORHAM MFG. CO.

Consisting of
Chafing Dish and Cover
Stand and Lamp
Hot Water Pan

Form, round
Finish, polished
Handles, ivory

Reed Birds.

MELT four pats of butter in Chafing Dish and let it become hot; put in one dozen birds and cook ten minutes over hot water, cover on. When finished, add to the gravy a tablespoonful of chopped parsley, salt to taste and serve.

Roast Beef Hash.

PUT in Chafing Dish four pats of butter and melt.
Mix one pound of finely chopped, cold roast beef,
and an equal quantity in bulk of finely chopped cold
boiled potatoes, moistened with one-half cup of bouillon; put in dish and cook over open fire until beef and
potatoes are well warmed through; season to taste,
sprinkle with a tablespoonful of finely chopped parsley,
and serve. A little chopped shives or onions can be
added, if desired, but should be first cooked with the
butter.

Roast Beef Deviled.

MAKE deviled sauce in Chafing Dish, as per recipe, put in two cupfuls of cold roast beef, cut in pieces about one inch square and one-half inch thick, cook over open fire until meat is heated through, being careful not to burn. Should sauce not be "hot" enough, add seasoning to taste.

Frankfurter and Cabbage.

PUT in Chafing Dish two cupfuls of cabbage, shaved with vegetable cutter very thin; cover with water, add a heaping teaspoonful of salt, boil fifteen minutes, then put in eight links of Frankfurter and boil ten minutes   If the cabbage is thoroughly cooked through, drain off the water and add two pats of butter, mix with the cabbage and serve.

Season with pepper and vinegar, if desired.

STERLING SILVER CHAFING DISH $\frac{925}{1000}$ FINE. No. 25.

CAPACITY THREE HALF PINTS.

MADE BY GORHAM MFG. CO.

Consisting of
Chafing Dish and Cover
Stand and Lamp
Hot Water Pan

Form, round
Finish, polished
Handles, ivory

Smelts in Butter.

MELT four pats of butter in Chafing Dish, over hot water pan, and when it becomes hot, add two teaspoonfuls of lemon juice, then put in twelve smelts, they first having been boned. Cook five minutes, turn and cook three minutes, add about a tablespoonful of chopped parsley. Season to taste and serve.

Sweetbreads Braised in Butter.

MELT three pats of butter in Chafing Dish, over open fire, and when hot, put two pairs of sweetbreads that have been blanched and skinned and cut in slices, cook for twenty minutes, being careful they do not burn. Season with salt, white pepper, parsley and serve.

Squab Braised.

MELT in Chafing Dish two pats of butter ; after it becomes hot, put in the two squabs prepared as for broiling. Cook for ten minutes over open fire, cover on, being careful not to burn. Season with pepper, salt and chopped parsley, serve and pour over the birds the gravy from the dish.

Succotash.

MELT three pats of butter in Chafing Dish over hot water, put in can of corn and can of Lima beans. The beans should be first washed in cold water and drained. Salt a little, keep stirring, and cook for ten minutes, or until corn and beans are heated through ; add salt and pepper as desired.

STERLING SILVER CHAFING DISH 925/1000 FINE, No. 30.

CAPACITY FIVE HALF PINTS.

MADE BY GORHAM MFG. CO.

Consisting of
Chafing Dish and Cover
Stand and Lamp
Hot Water Pan

Form, round
Finish, polished
Handles, ivory

Tripe, Stewed with Onions.

PUT three pats of butter in Chafing Dish, with two heaping teaspoonfuls of chopped onions; cook until well done; put in three cups of tripe, cut in dice pieces, add one cup of cream and mix. Cook over hot water for ten minutes, or until thoroughly heated through. Pepper and salt to taste. Serve plain or with toast.

Tripe with Tomatoes.

PUT three pats of butter in Chafing Dish and let
become thoroughly hot, when put in the solid
part of one two-pound can of tomatoes and three
cupfuls of tripe, cut in dice pieces, and one teaspoonful Worcestershire sauce. Cook over hot water for
ten minutes, season with pepper and salt to taste.

Breast of Turkey Braised.

MELT four pats of butter in Chafing Dish and let it become hot, put, in with the butter one half breast of an eight pound roasted or boiled turkey, in four pieces, first taking off the skin. Cook over open fire for six minutes, turn and cook five minutes, being careful not to burn. Season to taste and serve.

Turkey Stew.

MAKE white sauce as per recipe ; put in one pound of cold boiled or roast turkey, cut into large dice pieces and four medium cold boiled potatoes sliced. When turkey and potatoes are thoroughly warmed through, season to taste and serve. A little chopped parsley or shives may be added if desired.

To make turkey stew with curry, add heaping tea-spoonful of curry powder to above.

Turkey Hash.

PUT in Chafing Dish four pats of butter and melt; mix one pound of finely chopped, cold roast turkey and an equal quantity in bulk of finely chopped cold boiled potatoes, moistened with one-half cup of bouillon, put in dish and cook over open fire until turkey and potatoes are well warmed through. Season to taste, sprinkle with a tablespoonful of finely chopped parsley, and serve.

Legs of Turkey Deviled.

MAKE deviled sauce in Chafing Dish, as per recipe, put in uncooked second joints and drum sticks of two turkeys, boned, cook over hot water pan for fifteen minutes and finish over open fire for ten minutes, cover on, being careful not to burn.

If cold roast or boiled turkey are to be used, cook five minutes or until thoroughly heated through.

STERLING SILVER AND BRONZE CHAFING DISH No. 35.

CAPACITY FOUR HALF PINTS.

MADE BY GORHAM MFG. CO.

Consisting of
Chafing Dish and Cover
Stand and Lamp
Hot Water Pan

Form, round
Dish and Cover, sterling silver
Stand, bronze
Hot Water Pan and Lamp, copper

Veal Cutlets in Butter.

PUT three pats of butter in Chafing Dish, melt thoroughly, then put in two cutlets. Cutlets should be about three-quarters of an inch thick. Cook over hot water pan, cover on, for eight minutes, turn and cook five minutes. Season to taste and serve.

Veal Deviled.

MAKE deviled sauce in Chafing Dish as per recipe, put in two cupfuls of cold roast veal, cut into pieces about one inch square, and one half inch thick. Cook over open fire until meat is heated through, being careful not to burn. Should sauce not be "hot" enough, add seasoning to taste.

Venison Steak.

PUT three pats of butter in Chafing Dish, and let it melt, the steak should be about one inch thick, about one and one half pounds in weight, and nicely trimmed, put in dish with butter and cook over hot water, cover on, for ten minutes, then turn and cook five minutes. Salt and pepper as desired. When about done melt a little jelly in dish, and pour over the steak, or if preferred, jelly can be served with it.

Welsh Rarebit.

(Two Portions).

MELT three pats of butter in Chafing Dish over open fire, when thoroughly melted, put in three coffee cupfuls of grated (or cut in small pieces) American cream cheese, add about one-third of a pint of beer. Keep stirring. Put in about a teaspoonful of prepared English mustard When cheese is completely melted, add two beaten eggs, mix well and cook for a moment only. Salt to taste and serve on toast on hot plates.

BRONZE AND COPPER CHAFING DISH No. Y150.

CAPACITY FOUR HALF PINTS.

MADE BY GORHAM MFG. CO.

Consisting of
Chafing Dish and Cover
Stand and Lamp
Hot Water Pan

Form, round
Stand, bronze,
Dishes and Lamp, copper
Handle, ebony

Boiled White Fish.

CUT lengthwise from an eight pound fish, a piece large enough to cover the bottom of the Chafing Dish pan, put in water enough to just cover the fish, two teaspoonfuls of lemon juice or vinegar, two pats of butter and a little salt; boil about ten minutes, put on a platter and pour over it melted butter and chopped parsley. Serve with Graham bread.

White Sauce.

MIX in a bowl, three heaping teaspoonfuls of flour, with a pat of butter, add a little water and thin with milk or cream, put in dish over hot water pan. Salt to taste. Keep continually stirring and free from lumps, until thoroughly cooked; as it thickens, add milk or cream until the proper consistency, when done, let it come to a boil for an instant, being careful not to burn.

As this sauce is used with every Newburgh, Fricassee, etc., be careful as to details.

The End

www.ingramcontent.com/pod-product-compliance
Lightning Source LLC
Chambersburg PA
CBHW011203090426
42742CB00019B/3396